BIG MACHINES FOR BIG JOBS

GARBAGE TRUCKS ON THE JOB

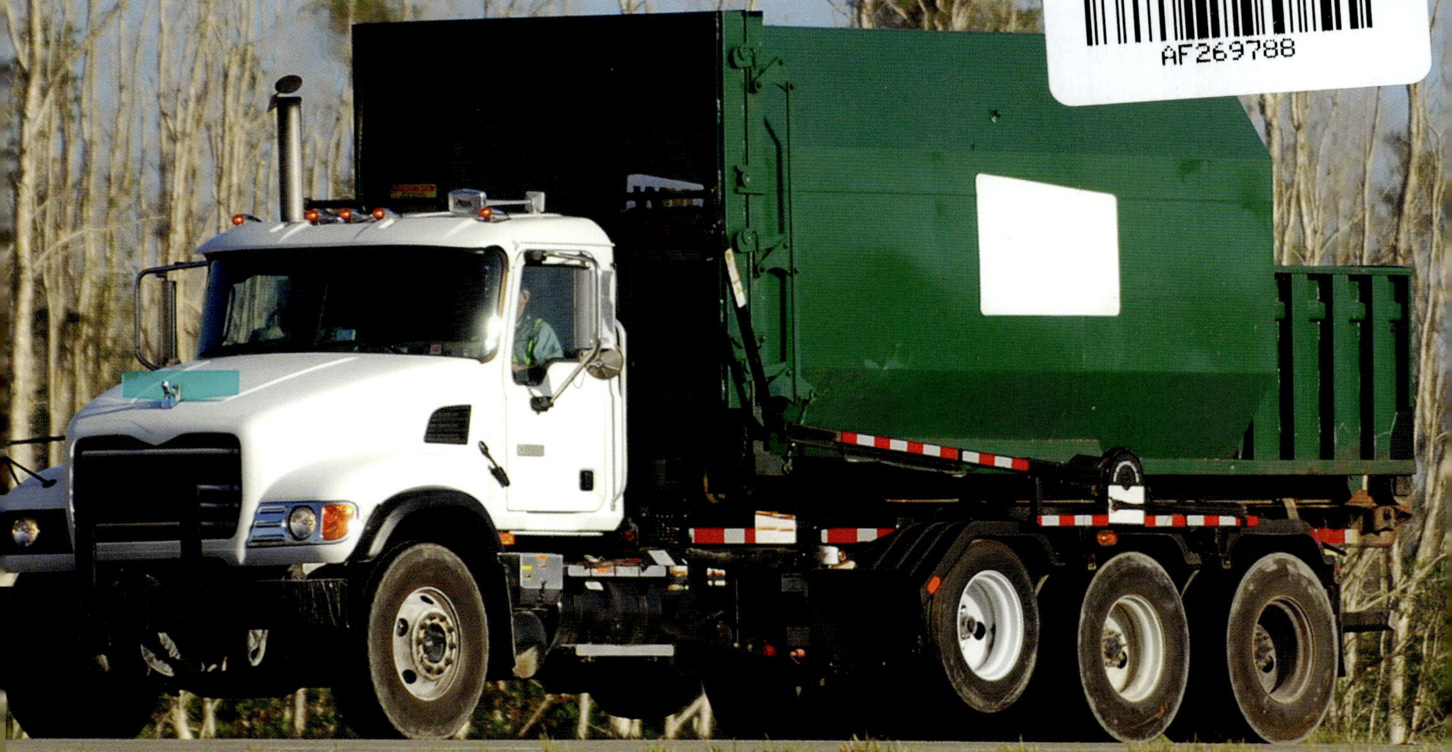

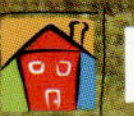

Norwood House Press

RYAN JAMES

Cataloging-in-Publication Data

Names: James, Ryan.
Title: Garbage trucks on the job / Ryan James.
Description: Buffalo, NY : Norwood House Press, 2026. | Series: Big machines for big jobs | Includes glossary and index.
Identifiers: ISBN 9781978573871 (pbk.) | ISBN 9781978573888 (library bound) | ISBN 9781978573895 (ebook)
Subjects: LCSH: Refuse collection vehicles--Juvenile literature. | Refuse collection--Juvenile literature.
Classification: LCC TD794.J359 2026 | DDC 628.4'420284--dc23

Published in 2026 by
Norwood House Press
2544 Clinton Street
Buffalo, NY 14224

Copyright © 2026 Norwood House Press
Designer: Rhea Magaro
Editor: Kim Thompson

Photo credits: Cover, p. 1 Ivan Cholakov/Shutterstock.com; p. 3 Jenya Smyk/Shutterstock.com; p. 5 Carolyn Franks/Shutterstock.com; p. 6, 17 Virrage Images/Shutterstock.com; p. 7 Nadya So/Shutterstock.com; p. 9 Karolis Kavolelis/Shutterstock.com; p. 10 trekandshoot/Shutterstock.com; p. 12 Henk Vrieselaar/Shutterstock.com; p. 13 Dalibor Danilovic/Shutterstock.com; p. 14 Victor Yarmolyuk/Shutterstock.com; p. 15 BrandonKleinPhoto/Shutterstock.com; p. 18, 19 Noel V. Baebler/Shutterstock.com; p. 21 Matt Gush/Shutterstock.com;

Printed in the United States of America

Some of the images in this book illustrate individuals who are models. The depictions do not imply actual situations or events.

CPSIA compliance information: Batch #CSNHP26: For further information contact Norwood House Press at 1-800-237-9932.

Find us on 

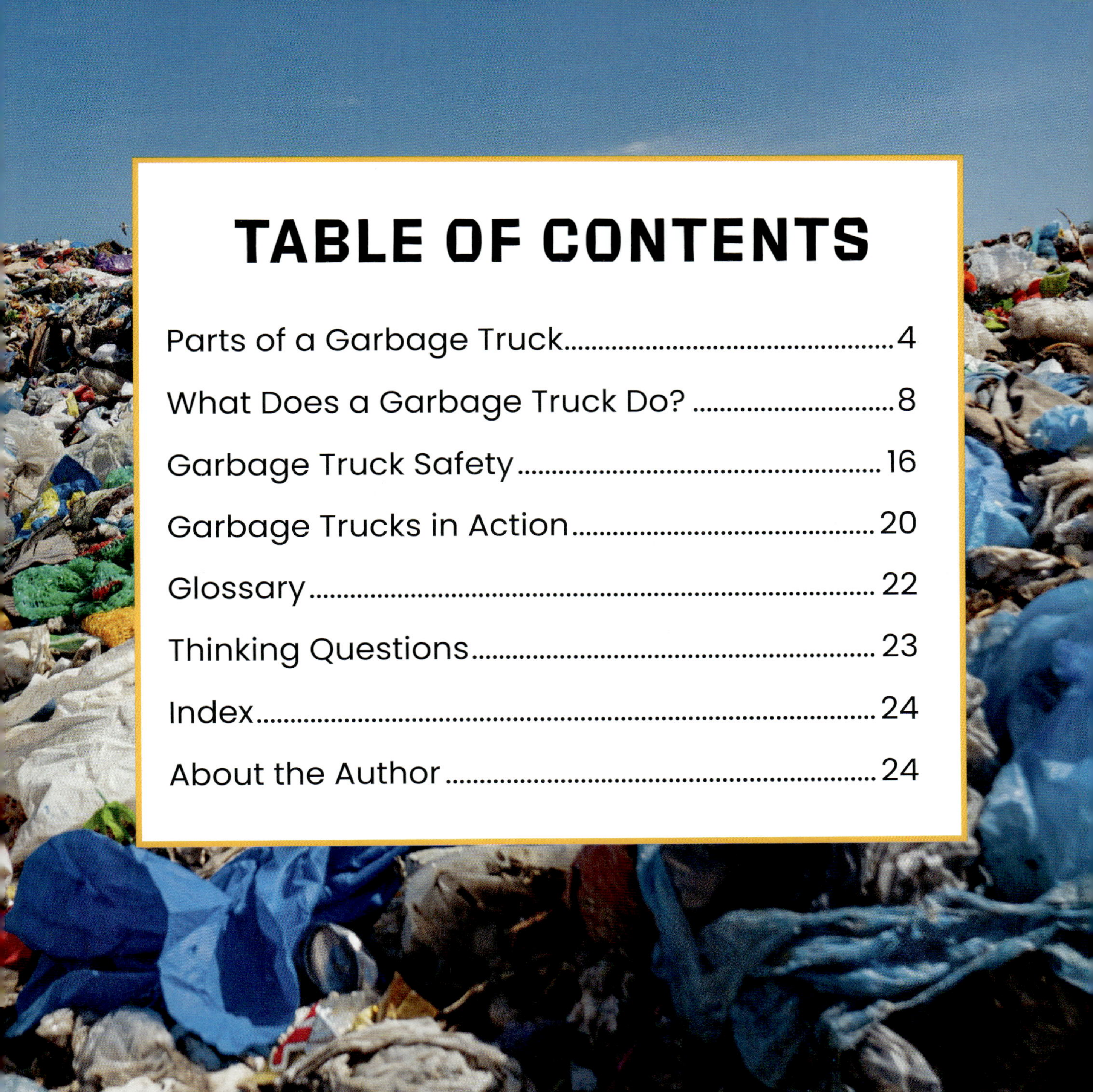

TABLE OF CONTENTS

PARTS OF A GARBAGE TRUCK

Garbage trucks are big machines.

Big wheels help them move.

A garbage truck has a cab.

The **operator** sits there.

The truck has moving arms. It has a **hopper**. The **tailgate** is in the back.

WHAT DOES A GARBAGE TRUCK DO?

Garbage trucks follow a **route**. They pick up trash from homes. They pick up trash from **businesses**.

SLOW DOWN
25DN-023
McNeilus
M.3
CAUTION WIDE TURNS

The operator **controls** the arms. The arms pick up bins. They dump trash into the hopper.

The hopper pushes the trash into the truck. A **compactor** squeezes the trash. Then, more trash will fit in.

The truck takes the garbage to a **landfill**. The trash spills out the tailgate.

There are different kinds of garbage trucks. Side loaders pick up bins from the side. Front loaders pick up bins from the front.

Some back loaders do not have moving arms. Workers must pick up bins with their hands. They dump the trash into the back.

GARBAGE TRUCK SAFETY

It is important to be safe around garbage trucks. You should stay with an adult.

Do not go near a truck when it is working. Let the operators do their jobs.

Never touch the truck's moving arms.

They might hurt you.

GARBAGE TRUCKS IN ACTION

Garbage trucks are **vehicles** on the job. They keep neighborhoods clean every day!

2237
CLEAN AIR VEHICLE
POWERED BY NATURAL GAS
REP
SE
republic
925-6
2237
PACHECO, CA
CA553

GLOSSARY

businesses (BIZ-ni-ses): companies that make or sell products and services, such as stores and factories

compactor (kuhm-PAKT-ur): a machine that presses or crushes something to make it take up less space

controls (kuhn-TROHLZ): makes a machine work by pushing buttons and moving levers and switches

hopper (HAH-pur): the area of a garbage truck where the trash gets dumped in

landfill (LAND-fil): a large area where garbage is buried

operator (AH-puh-ray-tur): a person whose job is to work a machine

route (rout): the path a garbage truck follows to pick up trash from homes and businesses

tailgate (TALE-gayt): a gate at the back of a vehicle that can be folded down for loading and unloading

vehicles (VEE-i-kuhlz): machines used to move people or things from one place to another

THINKING QUESTIONS

1. What is the job of a garbage truck?

2. How is each type of garbage truck different from the others?

3. Where does a garbage truck go after it picks up all the garbage?

4. How can you stay safe around a garbage truck?

5. Why are garbage trucks important?

INDEX

ABOUT THE AUTHOR

Ryan James lives in the mountains of North Carolina where he goes hiking with his dog Bailey. He loves fly fishing, visiting farms in the area, and picking fresh produce. He has always enjoyed writing and wrote his first book as a teenager.